LEEDS COLLEGE OF ART
BLENHEIM WALK LIBRARY

D0182474

LEEDS COL OF ART & DESIGN
R56295P0084

LISSON GALLERY

Shirazeh Houshiary

A Suite for Shirazeh Houshiary

Jacopo Pontormo
The Annuciation, c.1527
Fresco
Santa Felicita, Florence, Italy

The form is the possibility of the structure.
(Ludwig Wittgenstein)

In my work the form is definitely not a point of departure, but of arrival. The [art] object is the instrument through which an image asserts itself, it is a creative experience which is not born of the form but which reveals itself through the form.
(SH)

1 Studio: Point of departure; Point of arrival

The most ascetic art, striving modestly and with few resources to attain to the most exalted regions of thought and feeling, is not only borne along by the matter which it has sworn to repudiate, but is nourished and sustained by it as well. Without matter art could not exist; without matter art would be something it never once desired to be. Whatever renunciation art makes of matter merely bears witness anew to the impossibility of its escape from this magnificent, this unequivocal bondage.
(Henri Focillon)

Where is the painting? To ask the question is to beg many answers. We say: it is on the canvas (or the panel, or the wall): but *what* is on the support? It is matter, without doubt. The painting is in the matter: it is a material thing. The support is material; we see it as such, in this case, the warp and weft of the canvas (in others the grain or solidity of the wood, the abraded and cracked plaster of the wall). The paint itself is material. In the case of fresco the pigment is embedded in the support. The painting is on (or in) the support. This is the first answer, the answer is true, and what is true is important. (When we speak of art and its being, we are properly enjoined to deal with matters of probity.) It is also banal. There are complications and variants: in the paintings with which we are here concerned, the paint (aquacryl) is laid on to the canvas in many layers, eliminating the memory of the canvas weave, the painted surface perfected to pure light or pure darkness by many applications, many rubbings down, like lacquer; the marks are inscribed in pencil, a kind of writing, intimately and infinitely repetitive, spun like spider's silk from the centre on to the perfect skin of paint, a dust cloud, a constellation.

The object is placed on the wall. We say, 'we contemplate the object', but, we should say, more exactly, we *look* at the object, we *see* the object. It is the painting we contemplate. But the painting is not the object; neither is the painting an emanation of the object. The painting is experienced between the support and the eye, between the object and the receiving intelligence. Take away the object and the painting will disappear. The object is the necessary occasion of the painting. Take away the painting and the object remains. 'Painting consists of material hellishly woven, ephemeral and of little worth,' wrote Jacopo Pontormo to a friend, 'because if the superficial coating is removed, nobody any longer pays any attention to it.' The arena is not the performance; the floor is not the dance.

In order to contemplate the painting we need the object, which is the support and that which has been placed on it (or in it). But the object which is the material support and the material placed on it is not the painting. The painting – the work – is what occurs between the phenomenal material actualities of support, pigment and mark and the phenomenological realities of perception, conception, cognition, recognition, and feeling. What is experienced is the emanation of the painting. What is experienced is the work. The painting is made in the material – *embodied* – act of contemplation. In these works, this is true in the case of both the artist and the contemplative observer.

Afternoon light fades in the studio. The February sky over Wandsworth pales in subtleties of pale blue, grey, silver, dull white. The painting at the far end of the plain industrial space – *Black Light* – intensifies its effects in subtle response to the changing light. A thousand, thousand white marks, a cosmic dust composed of a single word, register the fugitive moments of departing day-light, the gradual augmentation of circumambient shadow, as a lucent glow emerging from thickening darkness. *Lux in tenebris*. Contemplating this phenomenon the mind is absorbed into a prolonged act of attention. Looking and breathing become being. What is contingent and beautiful is not only the receding light of the dusk, another day's brightness becoming twilight, but the disposition of walls and windows, white surfaces for light, clear panes to admit it. What is contingent fades with the light; the painting's radiance, not contingent, not beautiful, gleams, an emanation in the dusk, like a white shadow. Attention concentrates into a moment of ecstasy. For a moment the river that flows below the windows, its dappled ripples and currents, its streaming weeds, its flashing fish and fowl, is forgot.

Jacopo Pontormo
The Deposition of Christ, 1525–28
Panel
Santa Felicita, Florence, Italy

2 Panel, Wall and Window

An artist is someone who is capable of unveiling the invisible, not a producer of art objects.
(SH)

In the church of Santa Felicita in Florence, close by the south foot of the Ponte Vecchio, are two works by Jacopo Pontormo: the strange and magisterial *Deposition* (oil on panel) and a wonderful, mercurial fresco of the *Annunciation*. Both are known well by Shirazeh Houshiary, and important to her as an artist; while making her recent work they have been important objects of her contemplation and recollection. The essence of what it is that

Angelico, Fra (Guido di Pietro)
The Annunciation, 1442
Fresco/Cell 3
Museo di San Marco dell'Angelico,
Florence, Italy

travels between art works over time and between settings and situations is nothing to do with style (where there is no expressive intention, style is of no significance) or medium (media change with circumstances): it is found, rather, in rhythm, abstract forms, the dynamics of inner structures, indwelling spirit, feeling; things that persist regardless of material contingencies.

The *Deposition* is composed of a descending dynamic swirling spiral of figures, the colours of their garments luminous and iridescent, subtly-glowing aerial hues of pink, blue, orange, verdigris. There is nowhere a sign of material support: they appear as if suspended weightless in the air, as if the never-to-be repeated, ever-to-be-repeated act of grace – an act of lifting and lowering the weight of an inert body – were in this unique case of such a kind as to suspend the laws of gravity and of time. Weightless, immaterial, entranced out of time and place, beyond contingency, in *exstasis*, these figures are caught in a kind of now-outward-facing, now-inward-facing, doubly-helical dance. The iridescent colours of Houshiary's most recent towers derive from those in Pontormo's *Deposition:* in both the towers and the painting, in Wittgenstein's phrase, 'the structure of the atomic fact' is similar, it is the configurations that change, are variable.

The *Annunciation* is similarly extraordinary. In a device unprecedented in Florentine painting, the Angelic Colloquy – the miraculous encounter of Gabriel with Mary – is here removed from the fictive time and place of *quattrocento* pictorial representation, to enter the moment of the spectator's immediate space. Without premonition, her foot rising to the first step of a stair, the Virgin, hearing a sound, half-turns; the sound is of an archangel assuming the condition of visibility. We see him as she sees him, an amazing winged figure spinning out of aerial vacancy into a momentary materiality. We know that this instantiation of material form is real, for his face and garments catch the light from his left, as do hers, likewise, from her right. Both figures are caught in dynamic but subtle *contrapposto*, spirally turning as upon a vertical axis: conceptually they form a double helix. Between girl and archangel, and above them, in Pontormo's astounding original conception, a real window, through whose clear panes shines that natural light which touches them both with radiance.

Art speaks to art over time and through space. Contingent and beautiful, elemental light, appropriated by art, becomes at once reality and metaphor, material energy and ethereal sign, phenomenal and phenomenological. Perceived by the eye, received by the intelligence, known before and recognised again, that white light of Pontormo's window, we may say, shines through another window in another city (and through a thousand, thousand windows in innumerable cities). The device of art is not the art: the object, the support and medium, is not the painting; the configuration of modules is not the sculpture. Like the painting and the sculpture, the window is the instrument through which an image asserts itself.

To contemplate the light we need the window that directs it into the place of contemplation. The art is not the glass and the ingenious engineered tracery that holds it in place, it is a creative experience which is not born of the form but which reveals itself through the form. It is attention that concentrates lines and light into meaning. For the moment of that contemplative concentration, transported by light thus configured, the quotidian traffic of St Martin's Lane and Trafalgar Square, the pictures in the galleries opposite, the city's ceaseless clatter of sound and movement, what goes on in the world, is forgot.

Study for Constantin Brancusi
Endless Column
Fountain pen on photograph
of the 'Hay Market' site
in Tirgu Jiu, Romania

O body swayed to music, O brightening glance,
How can we know the dancer from the dance?
(W.B. Yeats)

It is an architectural diagram of dance. The dance is in the architectonic: as in the invisible structure of a piece of music. Structure here as in Wittgenstein's thrilling sequence of propositions:

Space, time and colour (colouredness) are forms of objects.
Only if there are objects can there be a fixed form of the world.
The fixed, the existent and the object are one.
The object is the fixed, the existent; the configuration is the changing, the variable.
The configuration of the objects forms the atomic fact.
In the atomic fact objects hang one in another, like the links of a chain.
In the atomic fact the objects are combined in a definite way.
The way in which objects hang together in the atomic fact is the structure of the atomic fact.
The form is the possibility of the structure.

The towers work on the receiving imagination by way of enacted oppositions:

A multiple of spirals, in two rhythms, one clockwise and one anti-clockwise, around a vertical axis created of coloured or white anodised aluminium cellular modules presents infinite diversities of configuration to the eye as the body moves in relation to it: simplicity, complexity; movement, stillness;

The tower is finite, an atomic fact – 'an atomic fact is a combination of objects (entities, things)' – but potentially and in principle endless, structurally infinite. Wittgenstein elaborates: 'Even if the world is infinitely complex, so that every fact consists of an infinite number of atomic facts and every atomic fact is composed of a number of objects, even then there must be objects and atomic facts.' Each tower is at once what it is and an image of its own potential extension to infinity;

Seen from a distance the reticulated form is perceived as transparent, diaphanous – 'through which light shines' – or as a twisting veil, the material elements caught up in the air and light, the air and light caught up in its fabric, as if the architectonic were an emanation of the surrounding space: it spins as if out of vacancy into being! Approach closely, look obliquely, and the proximity of the modules to each other creates a density to the eye, a kind of complex opacity, as if the kinetic energies of the indwelling structure had fused into an object, as if the structure had revealed 'the possibility' of form, as if a force had evolved a solid form.

It is the 'space, time and colouredness' within Houshiary's spiralling towers that is the form made possible by the structure. The tower is the instrument through which an image asserts itself: the configured space within is itself the dynamic aerial image. This creative experience of a dynamic image manifest in the absence of form is precisely that which reveals itself through the form. Air, light and space are the primary materials of the work. The sculptural object – the visible tower – is a means to an end: the configuration of space; just as is the window's steel tracery is a means to the configuration of light. The *structure* of the dance is invisible, immaterial, known only at the moment of the dance; all that is required for its execution is the architecture through which it reveals itself; as musician and instrument reveal the structure of the music, and the weaving dancers reveal, in turning steps and figures, the architectonics of the dance.

{A digression ('a sideways step'): 'The way in which objects hang together in the atomic fact is the structure of the atomic fact' and 'the form is the possibility of the structure' are propositions that would have been well understood by Brancusi, whose *endless columns* are the most significant artistic precursors to Houshiary's towers. (Art speaks to art over time and through space.) His first sketched projection for the *Endless Column*, drawn by fountain pen on a photograph of the 'Hay Market' site in Tirgu Jiu, conceived of the work as a double-helix. The modular ascent of the actual column, not so much 'like links in a chain' as like octagonal beads threaded on a central vertical axis, is paradoxically sustained by gravity: an enacted opposition. (When asked, what was the column for? Brancusi replied: 'to hold up the vault of heaven'!)}

4 Light: The emanation of the object

There is indeed the inexpressible. This shows itself, it is the mystical.
(Wittgenstein)

At the heart of the spiralling cloud, roughly rectangular in configuration, light shines out; at the edges the cloud attenuates and fragments into perfect blackness. In *Veil*, a small painting from 2003, this window-shaped cloud of dispersing or imploding light, of a thousand, thousand written marks, hangs in space like the object that gives it its title. Paradoxically, light concentrates where there is the thickest concentration of material marks. It is not so

Angelico, Fra (Guido di Pietro)
The Annunciation, *c.*1438–45
Fresco
Museo di San Marco dell'Angelico,
Florence, Italy

Francisco de Zurbaran
The Veil of Veronica, 1631–36
Oil on canvas
51.5 × 71 cm
The National Museum of Fine Arts, Stockholm

much an object as an emanation of light. 'Veil' here might signify, paradoxically, a radiance that obscures, as if what might be seen is hidden behind a veil of light, or as if a window of bright white light were a phenomenal manifestation of what is invisible (i.e. *not* a symbol). The image is received by the eye: 'I believe what I see; only what I see!' says the artist. She means something more than the simple empiricism implied. 'What *can* be shown *cannot* be said' said Wittgenstein. It is through what can be shown that the art within art transmigrates across time.

In the Convent of San Marco, in Florence, there are two fresco paintings, by Fra Angelico, of the Annunciation; they are known well to Houshiary and important to her; in the preparation of recent work, they have been objects of her contemplation and recollection. In the painting in cell no. 3 on the upper floor, the Virgin assumes the posture and gesture appropriate to what was known as the 'praiseworthy condition of submission': she accepts her fate with humility. It is more direct, less circumstantial an event than that represented by the great *Annunciation*, which vision, revealed at the turn of the stairs to the cells, was meant to concentrate the minds of those who, after supper, ascend to solitude. (These representations of the Virgin in the condition called *Humiliatio* are far removed from that of Pontormo's innocent barefoot girl: Fra Angelico's Virgin is already beatified as her halo attests.) No words can utter the inexpressible: the ineffable wonder of this Colloquy is beyond speech. Within this vaulted loggia a perfect arch connects Mary with Gabriel: both are contained, conjoined within the visible architecture of the moment; kneeling and bowing, the girl half-turns in tune with the architectonic, and at the heart of this dynamic structure a marvellous light illuminates the space and the enclosing walls. That it is real, this light, cannot be doubted: both archangel and virgin cast shadows.

What is the light? It is a painted thing: the painting is in the matter, embedded in the material support, the cracked and abraded plaster of the wall. Without the wall there is no painting. This emanation of light is not the painting. The light is the form made possible by the structure: the painting embedded in the wall is the instrument through which the image asserts itself, projecting an experience of light into the cell. In this case, the loggia and its walls are marvellously an image of the cell; the plaster is miraculously that of the wall of both loggia and cell, the setting of the angelic mission and the place in which it is contemplated: consubstantial. To contemplate this light required the painting which directs it into the place of contemplation.

Air, light and space are the primary materials of Houshiary's recent work; they are the elements by means of which the invisible is unveiled. They are brought into being by that prolonged, repetitive, contemplative writing of a word (the sign of a breath) into a perfect surface space that bears no trace of its supporting material, as if it might itself be light or darkness out of which darkness or light are conjured. It is the material act that generates the immaterial effect, the emanation. It is the light or colour shimmer, or darkness thus generated by a structure (in each painting unique, discovered in the unrepeatable action) of objects – the innumerable strokes of the pencil – combined in a definite way, hanging together in a definite way – that generates the form. This is the configuration of objects that forms the atomic fact, which can be no other. Contemplating this phenomenal emanation the mind is absorbed into a prolonged act of attention. The form is the focus of this contemplation that concentrates the mind. That is what these paintings are for.

Kazimir Malevich
Suprematist Painting (White Planes in Dissolution), 1917–18
Oil on canvas
97 × 70 cm
Stedelijk Museum, Amsterdam

Do not these forms that live in space and matter live first in the mind? (Focillon)

What it is that recurs in art works over time and between diverse circumstances is found, in material terms, in abstract forms and the dynamics of inner structures, and also in intangibilities more difficult of analysis, vibrancies of spirit and feeling: both are aspects of what Focillon called 'the life of forms in art.' They are things that persist regardless of the changing circumstances of purpose, subject, theme and meaning. Form thus considered is a thing of the mind that finds expression in matter. 'Without matter art could not exist; without matter art would be something it never once desired to be.' There are histories in art, ancient and modern, as in real life, since consciousness began, of a longing for escape 'from this magnificent, this unequivocal bondage'. It is an impossible dream. Thinking of Malevich, Mondrian, Klee and Klein, among many others, Gottfried Boehm wrote: 'The dream of the absolute: it was and is something totally real. One can call it the dream of the twentieth century…' It is a dream of recurrence.

'The square of the Suprematists', wrote Malevich, 'can be compared to the symbols of primitive men. It was not their intent to produce ornaments but to express the feelings of rhythm.' To express the feelings of rhythm is to bring into visibility or tangibility – contemplation or dance – the first actuality of life, which is breath: to re-enact the cyclic dynamic between the body and the world. Malevich's astonishing 'white on white' drawings for his manifesto, *The Non-Objective World*, enact the fading from self when, as in a dream, what goes on in the world is forgot. In his art, as in that of Houshiary, it is what cannot be seen that matters, the ceaseless rhythm and energy within things, invisible but ever-present in the perceptible world: it is its animation, its inspiration and expiration, the energy that is independent of the objects through which it moves. In *Suprematism (White on White)* the material image strives towards its own dissolution, towards invisibility, white fading into white. Its renunciation of all but white confirms the materiality of light. It is an art that unveils the invisible. In Houshiary's film, *Veil*, a swarm of points of white light configures as light-in-darkness, glows out and fades away, enacts inspiration and expiration; in *Shroud*, a thousand, thousand points of pink and white colour-light shimmer in the rhythms of breath, a lucent glow emerges from white light, fades into white light: it is a fact as real as the white on white of the face in Zurbaran's amazing painting, a work important to Houshiary.

In the *Annunciata* of Antonello da Messina the Virgin is transfigured: the blue of her veil shines out of the surrounding black; from within the heart-shaped opening of her veil – a kind of window – her face shines with a paler light. (The simply-carpentered worn reading desk and book are minimal reminders of the contingent time out of which she has been removed by grace.) Several of Houshiary's most recent paintings – *Quiver*, *Fracture*, *Brittle Moment* – manifest in colour and feeling an active engagement with this marvellous painting. From an absolute darkness a fact emerges: a form is structured in a definite way, space, time and colour are components of this form. In Houshiary's paintings, as in Antonello's (in a quite different way), facture – the outcome of a methodology, what emerges from a *modus* of making – is invisible; it disguises (veils) the contingencies of medium and support to bring clarity and immediacy to its presentation. Above all, it is *Presence*, which in its title and in its essential form, determined by a definite structure, recollects the essential spirit of Antonello's great work: what is revealed is concealed, what is concealed is revealed, and, in Houshiary's own paradoxical formulation, what is unveiled is what was invisible.

Mel Gooding, April/May, 2008

Antonello da Messina
Our Lady of the Annunciation,
c. 1475–76
Tempera and oil on canvas
45 × 34.5 cm
Galleria Regionale della Sicilia
di Palazzo Abatellis, Palermo, Italy

Notes and references: ——— Wittgenstein is quoted from *Tractatus Logico-Philosophicus* (trans. C.K.Ogden, Routledge and Kegan Paul, London, 1922). Propositions, in order of quotation: 2.033, 2.0251–2.033, 4.2211, 6.522, 4.1212 (all italics as in original). Henri Focillon is quoted from *The Life of Forms in Art*, chapters III and IV (trans. C.B.Hogan and G. Kubler, Yale University Press, New Haven, 1942). W.B.Yeats is quoted from his poem, 'Among School Children'. For an account of the mysteries of the Annunciation and of the 'Angelic Colloquy', see Michael Baxandall, *Painting and Experience in Fifteenth Century Italy* (Oxford University Press, 1972). 'Every force evolves a form' is a Celtic proverb. Malevich is quoted from Ludwig Hilberseimer's introduction to the English language of *The Non-Objective World* (Paul Theobald, Chicago, 1959). Gottfried Boehm is quoted from his introduction to *Dream of the Absolute*, an exhibition at Galerie Bayeler, Basel, 1994.

19

Installation
Lisson Gallery, London 2008

Black Light 2008
White pencil on black aquacryl
190 × 190 cm

Vein 2006
Blue and red pencil on white aquacryl, white gesso on canvas
190 × 190 cm

Untitled 2008
White pencil on black aquacryl on canvas
40 × 40 cm

Shroud 2008
Red and blue pencil on white aquacryl on canvas
70 × 70 cm

Brittle Moment 2007
Blue pencil on black and white aquacryl on canvas
190 × 190 cm

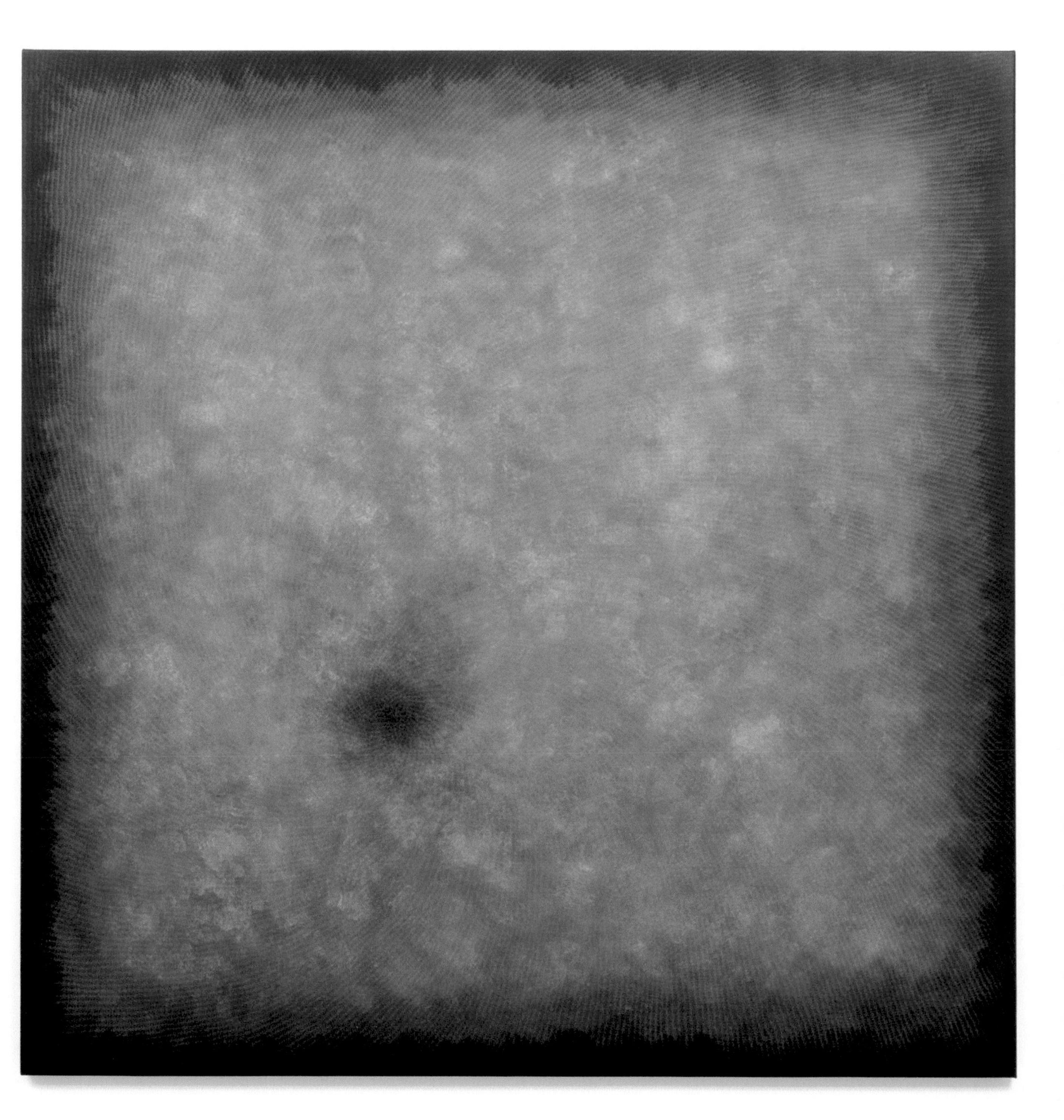

Flay 2008
Blue pencil on white and black aquacryl
190 × 190 cm

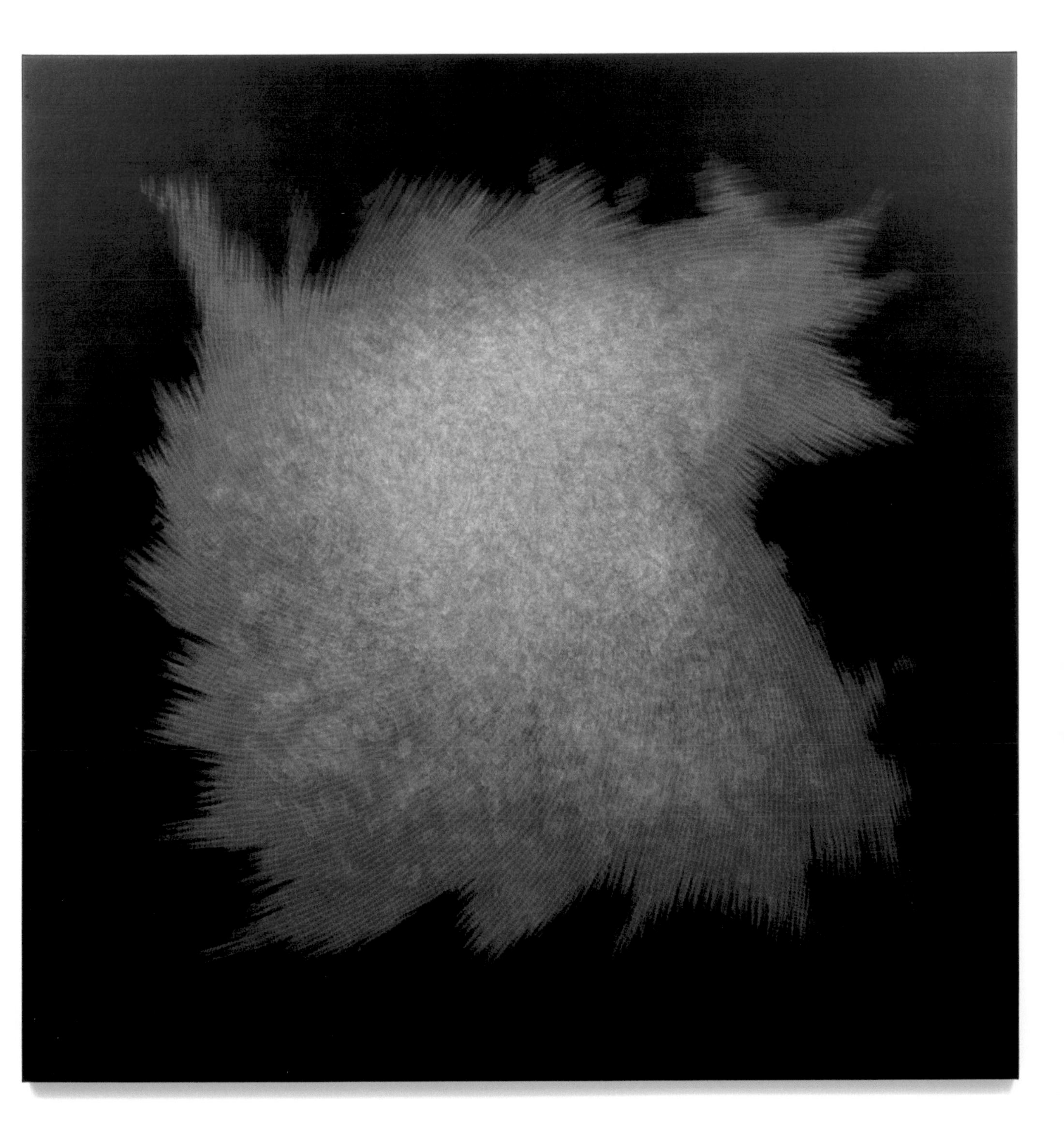

Untitled 2008
Blue and grey on black aquacryl on canvas
40 × 40 cm

Presence 2006 – 2007
Blue pencil on black aquacryl on canvas
190 × 190 cm

Thought 2007
Blue pencil on white aquacryl on canvas
190 × 190 cm

Quiver 2008
Blue pencil on black aquacryl on canvas
70 × 70 cm

Coalesce 2008
Blue pencil on white aquacryl on canvas
70 × 70 cm

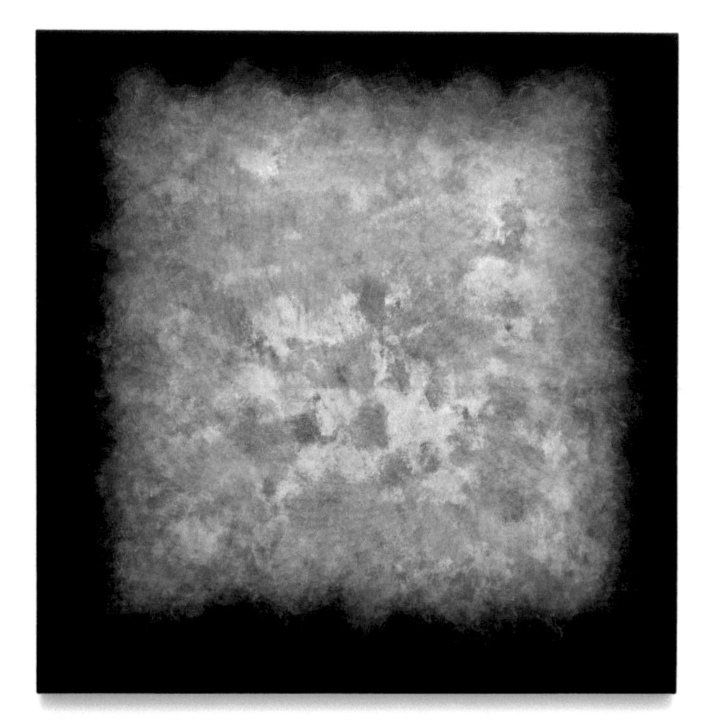

Isthmus 2007
Blue pencil on black acquacryl on canvas
70 × 70 cm

Lux 2008
Red and blue pencil on white aquacryl on canvas
70 × 70 cm

Signum 2008
Blue pencil on white aquacryl
100 × 100 cm

Fracture 2007
Blue and grey pencil on black and white aquacryl on canvas
190 × 190 cm

Relic 2008
Blue pencil on white aquacryl on canvas
70 × 70 cm

Flicker 2008
Blue and white pencil on black aquacryl on canvas
70 × 70 cm

Undoing the knot 2008
Anodized aluminum bricks and polished stainless steel
height 658 cm; ellipse 99 × 75 cm

White Shadow 2005
Aluminium bricks and steel cable
Height 405 cm; ellipse: 66 × 47 cm

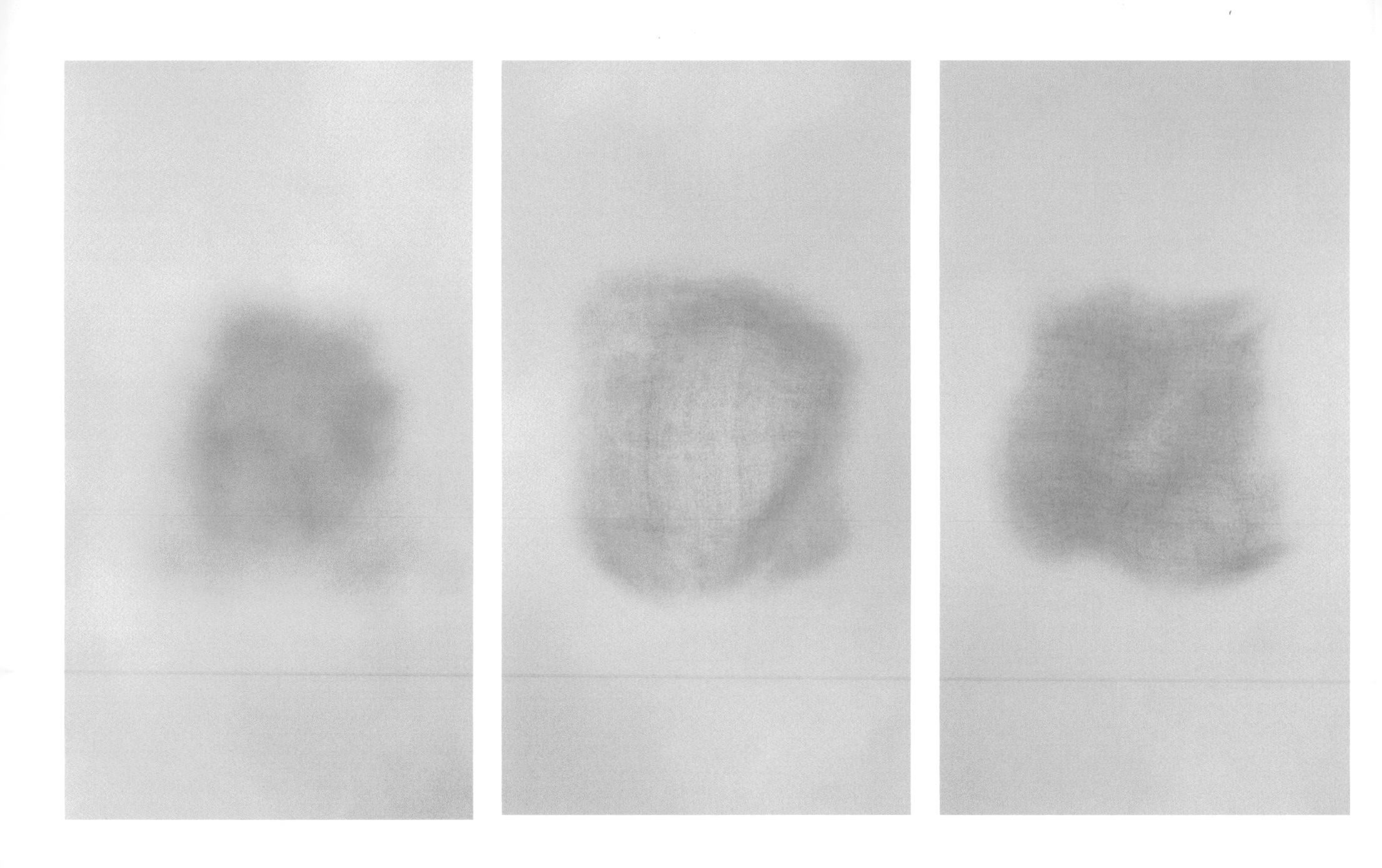

Shroud 2007
Animated Film
53 inch LCD Screen
ed.10+2AP

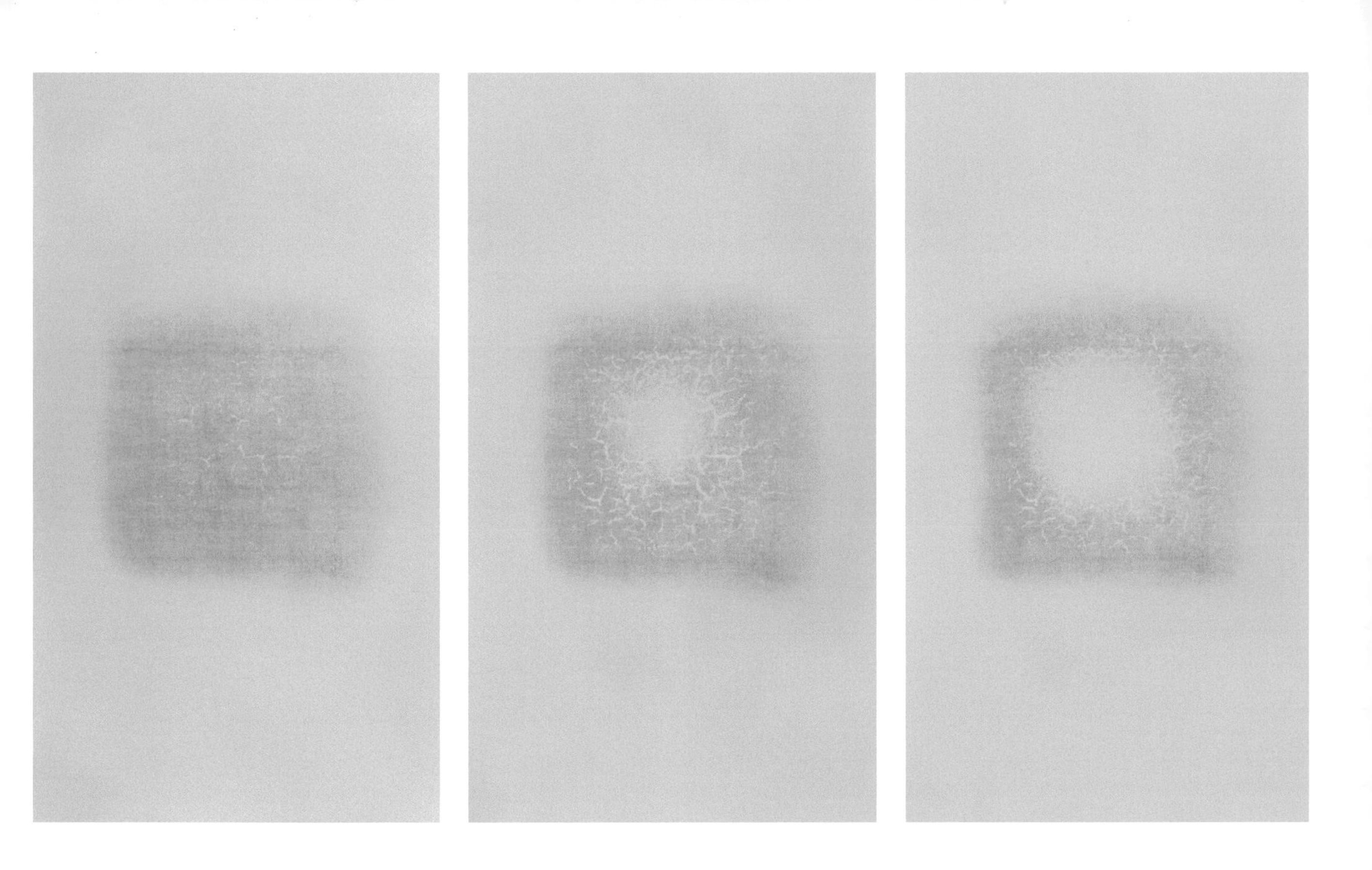

Veil 2005
Animated Film
variable
ed.6+2AP

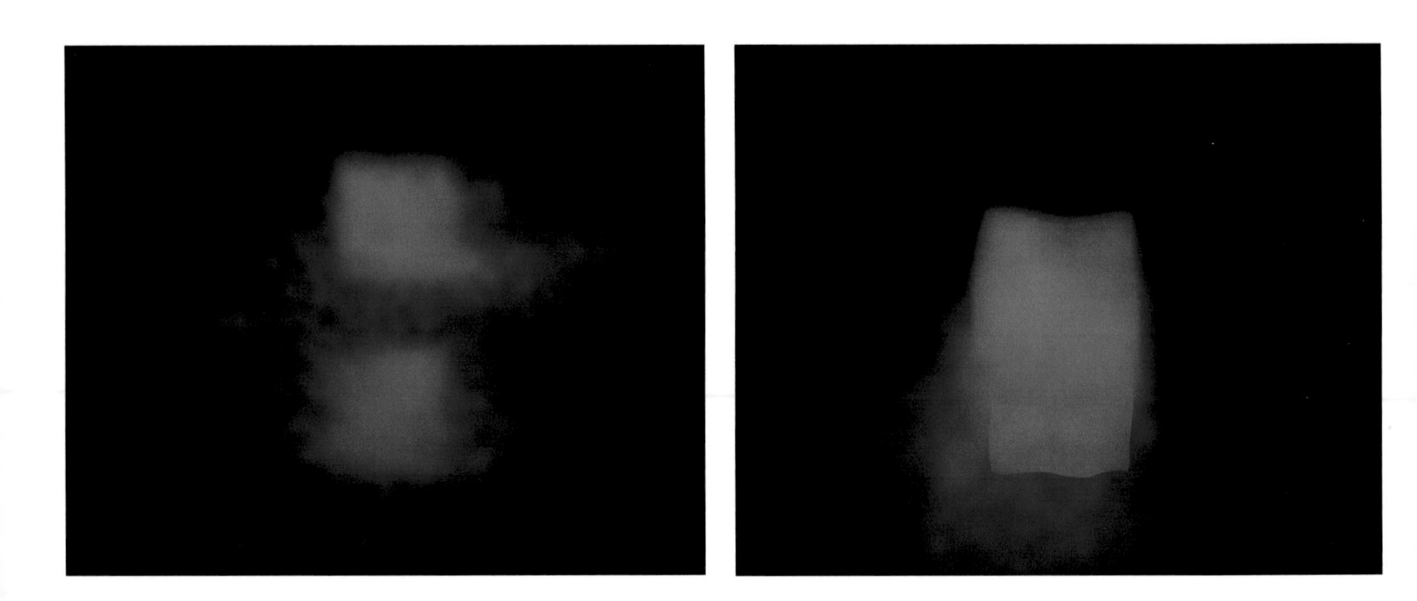

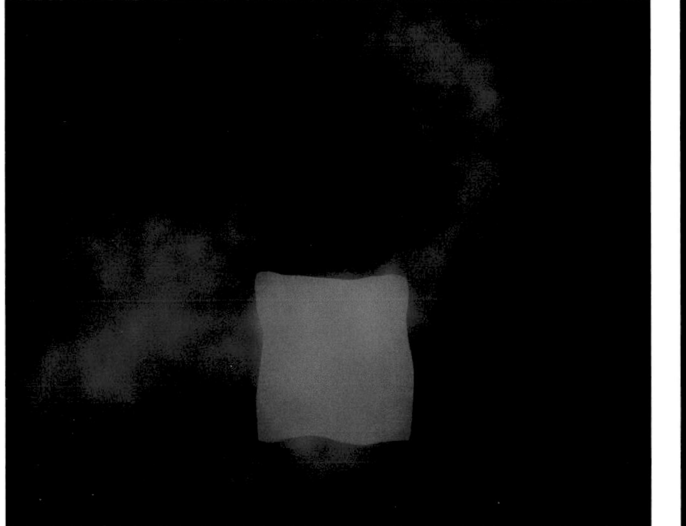

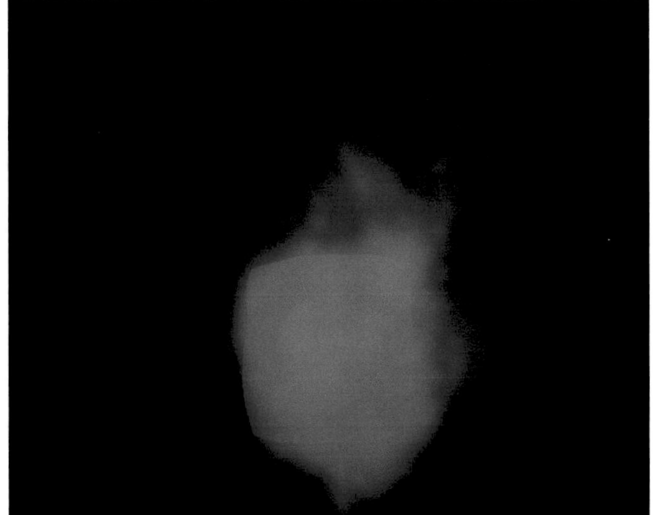

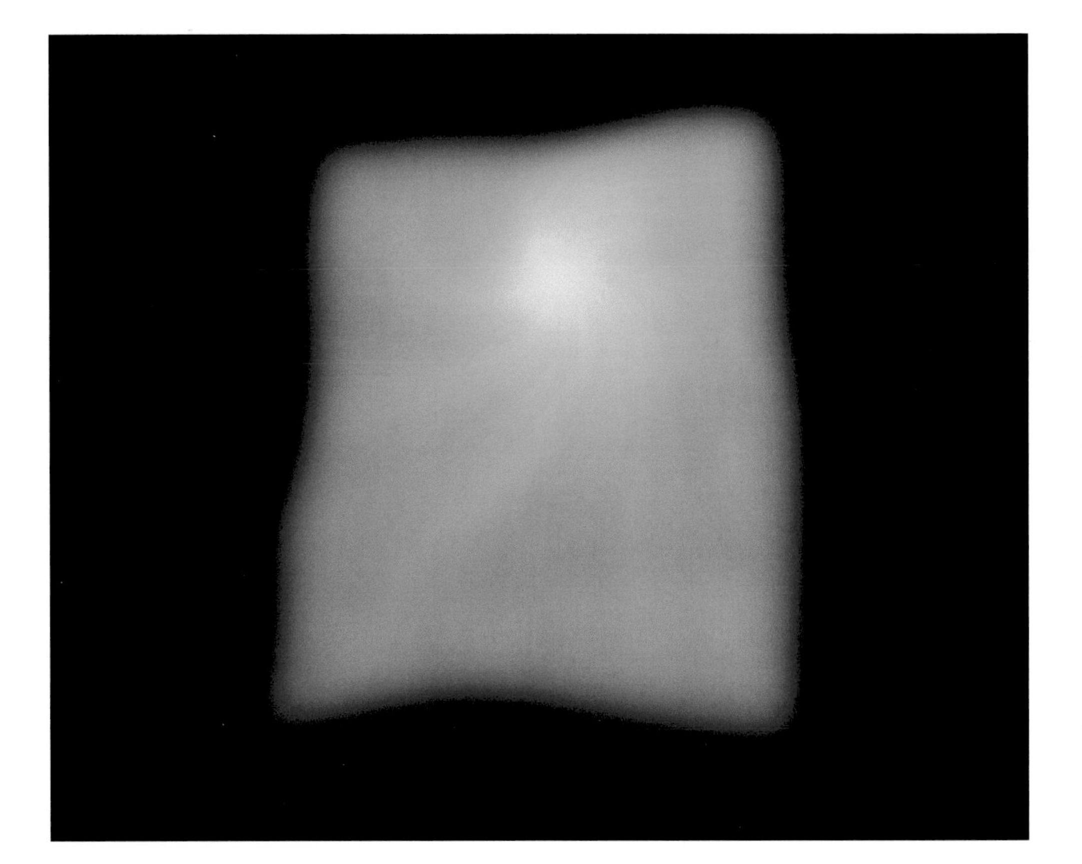

Commission for St Martin-in-the-Fields, London, 2008
Etched mouth blown clear glass and shot peened
stainless steel frame

Eclipse 2008
Anodized aluminum bricks and steel cable
Height 275 cm; ellipse 43 cm × 32 cm

List of illustrations

P.4
Jacopo Pontormo (1494–1556)
The Annuciation, c.1527
Fresco
Capponi Chapel, Santa Felicita, Florence, Italy
© 1990. Photo Scala, Florence

P.7
Jacopo Pontormo (1494–1556)
The Deposition of Christ, 1525–28
Panel
Capponi Chapel, Santa Felicita, Florence, Italy
© 2000. Photo Scala, Florence

P.8
Angelico, Fra (Guido di Pietro) (c.1387–1455)
The Annunciation, 1442
Fresco/Cell 3
Museo di San Marco dell'Angelico, Florence, Italy/
The Bridgeman Art Library

P.10
Study for Constantin Brancusi
Endless Column
Fountain pen on photograph
of the 'Hay Market' site
in Tirgu Jiu, Romania

P.13
Angelico, Fra (Guido di Pietro) (c.1387–1455)
The Annunciation, 1438 – 45
Fresco
Museo di San Marco dell'Angelico, Florence, Italy
© 1990. Photo Scala, Florence – Courtesy of The Ministerio
Beni e Att. Culturali

P.14
Francisco de Zurbaran (1598–1664)
The Veil of Veronica, 1631–36
Oil on canvas
51.5 × 71 cm
The National Museum of Fine Arts, Stockholm

P.16
Kazimir Malevich (1878–1935)
Suprematist Painting (White Planes in Dissolution), 1917–18
Oil on canvas
97 × 70 cm
Stedelijk Museum, Amsterdam

P.18
Antonello da Messina (c. 1430–1479)
Our Lady of the Annunciation, c. 1475–76
Tempera and oil on canvas
45 × 34.5 cm
Galleria Regionale della Sicilia di Palazzo Abatellis, Palermo, Italy

Plates

Photography: Dave Morgan

Pp.22–23
Installation
Lisson Gallery, London 2008

Pp.24–25
Black Light 2008
White pencil on black aquacryl
190 × 190 cm
Private Collection, Sydney

P.26
Vein 2006
Blue and red pencil on white aquacryl, white gesso on canvas
190 × 190 cm

P.27
Untitled 2008
White pencil on black aquacryl on canvas
40 × 40 cm

P.28
Shroud 2008
Red and blue pencil on white aquacryl on canvas
70 × 70 cm

P.29
Brittle Moment 2007
Blue pencil on black and white aquacryl on canvas
190 × 190 cm
Private Collection, Courtesy of Jeremy Lewison Ltd

Pp.30–31
Flay 2008
Blue pencil on white and black aquacryl
190 × 190 cm

P.32
Untitled 2008
Blue and grey on black aquacryl on canvas
40 × 40 cm

P.33
Presence 2006 – 2007
Blue pencil on black aquacryl on canvas
190 × 190 cm
Solomon R. Guggenheim Museum, New York
Purchased with funds contributed by the International Director's Council and Executive Committee and Sustaining Members, 2008

Pp.34–35
Thought 2007
Blue pencil on white aquacryl on canvas
190 × 190 cm

P.36
Quiver 2008
Blue pencil on black aquacryl on canvas
70 × 70 cm

Coalesce 2008
Blue pencil on white aquacryl on canvas
70 × 70 cm

P.37
Isthmus 2007
Blue pencil on black acquacryl on canvas
70 × 70 cm

P.38
Lux 2008
Red and blue pencil on white aquacryl on canvas
70 × 70 cm

P.39
Signum 2008
Blue pencil on white aquacryl
100 × 100 cm

P.40
Fracture 2007
Blue and grey pencil on black and white aquacryl on canvas
190 × 190 cm

P.41
Relic 2008
Blue pencil on white aquacryl on canvas
70 × 70 cm
Private Collection, USA

Flicker 2008
Blue and white pencil on black aquacryl on canvas
70 × 70 cm

Pp.42–43
Shirazeh Houshiary and Pip Horne
Undoing the knot 2008
Anodized aluminum bricks and polished stainless steel
height 658 cm; ellipse 99 × 75 cm

Pp.44–45
Shirazeh Houshiary and Pip Horne
White Shadow 2005
Aluminium bricks and steel cable
Height 405 cm; ellipse: 66 × 47 cm

Pp.46–47
Shroud 2007
Animated Film
53 inch LCD Screen
ed.10+2AP

Pp.48–49
Veil 2005
Animated Film
variable
ed.6+2AP

Pp.50–51
Shirazeh Houshiary and Pip Horne
Commission for St Martin-in-the-Fields, London, 2008
Etched mouth blown clear glass and shot peened stainless steel frame

P.52
Shirazeh Houshiary and Pip Horne
Eclipse 2008
Anodized aluminum bricks and steel cable
Height 275 cm; ellipse 43 × 32 cm

Acknowledgements

No exhibition can ever happen without the involvement of many people who put much care, attention and sensitivity into the making of it. If I have not mentioned their names here, I would like to thank them all.

My thanks go to Mark Hatchard who has been so patient and tireless with the laborious process of realising the two animations; Duncan McLeod for his precision in helping coordinate the show from the structural engineering of the sculpture towers to the presentation of the digital animations; Barry Goilleau of Benson/ Sedgwick Engineering who continues to excel with the fabrication of the tower pieces; and to the Rev. Nicholas Holtam, Vicar of St Martin in the Fields, and Vivien Lovell from Modus Operandi Art Consultants for their unwavering support of the East Window Commission and seeing it through.

My special thanks goes to Karolin Kober of the Lisson Gallery for her focus and dedication in the making of this catalogue and the show.

My deepest thanks goes to Mel Gooding who has written a wonderful text in which the experience of reading reveals the creative process of making art; and to Nicholas Logsdail for his continuing support. It is his interest and enthusiasm that has inspired me over the years and his friendship has been intelligent, true and clear.

And finally and in particular I thank Pip Horne for collaborating with me on so many of these projects and who understands the obsessiveness of the artist.

Colophon

Published on the occasion of Shirazeh Houshiary:
New Work, Lisson Gallery, 29 May–26 July, 2008

Published by Lisson Gallery
52–54 Bell Street
London NW1 5DA
T +44 (0)20 7724 2739
www.lissongallery.com

Lisson Gallery publication no. 50

Text: Mel Gooding

Editorial supervision:
Shirazeh Houshiary
Karolin Kober

Cover photograph: Ken Adlard
Photography: Dave Morgan
Photographic research: Justyna Niewiara

Design: A2/SW/HK

Printed by DeckersSnoeck

ISBN 978-3-86560-486-6

Distribution:

Europe
Verlag der Buchhandlung Walther König, Köln
Ehrenstr. 4, D-50672 Köln
Tel +49 (0) 221 / 20 59 6 – 53
Fax +49 (0) 221 / 20 59 6 – 60
Email: verlag@buchhandlung-walther-koenig.de

Switzerland
Buch 2000
c/o AVA Verlagsauslieferungen AG
Centralweg 16
CH-8910 Affoltern a.A.
Tel +41 (0) 1 762 42 00
Fax +41 (0) 1 762 42 10
a.koll@ava.ch

UK & Eire
Cornerhouse Publications
70 Oxford Street
GB–Manchester M1 5NH
Tel +44 (0) 161 200 15 03
Fax +44 (0) 161 200 15 04
publications@cornerhouse.org

Outside Europe
D.A.P. / Distributed Art Publishers, Inc.
155 6th Avenue, 2nd Floor
New York, NY 10013
Tel +1 212-627-1999
Fax +1 212-627-9484
eleshowitz@dapinc.com